Ron and Kim

by Pauline Cartwright
illustrated by Trish Hill

Harcourt
SCHOOL PUBLISHERS

ISBN 10: 0-15-351250-4
ISBN 13: 978-0-15-351250-6

Ordering Options
ISBN 10: 0-15-351211-3 (Grade 1 Advanced Collection)
ISBN 13: 978-0-15-351211-7 (Grade 1 Advanced Collection)
ISBN 10: 0-15-358018-6 (package of 5)
ISBN 13: 978-0-15-358018-5 (package of 5)

3 4 5 6 7 8 9 10   468   15 14 13 12 11 10 09 08

I have a mask for Sam.

Can you help me find a box,
Kim?

That box is much too big.

That box is much too little.

The pink box is good.

Surprise!
Here is a gift for you, Sam.

Thank you, Ron.
Look at me now!